Fencelines

Angela Hansen

A Publication of The Poetry Box®

Editing & Book Design by Shawn Aveningo Sanders
Cover Design by Shawn Aveningo Sanders
Cover Photo by Annie Spratt via Unsplash
Author Photo by Angela Rethwisch Photography

"Spring Thaw" and "Old Plow" were originally published in *Nebraska Life Magazine*.

ISBN: 978-1-956285-10-9
Printed in the United States of America.
Wholesale distribution via Ingram.

Published by The Poetry Box®, June 2022
Portland, Oregon
https://ThePoetryBox.com

To those who walk alongside me,
who remind me of my beauty, because of my scars.

To Sam, Leah, and Elaina — my entire world.
And to Scott — who broke down my walls and cherishes my worth.

Contents

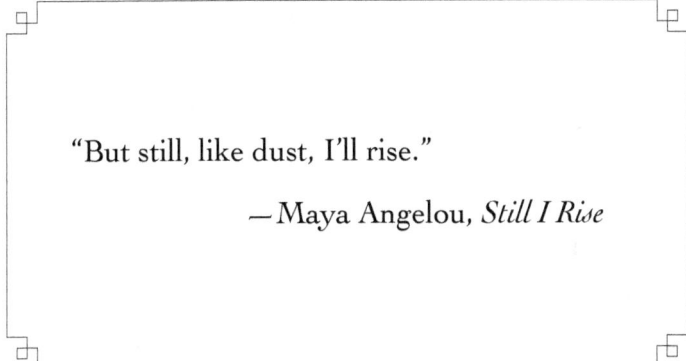

"But still, like dust, I'll rise."

—Maya Angelou, *Still I Rise*

Along the Banks of Deer Creek

Winter lays weary beside the creek,
her bony spine pressed into the hillside.
The wind tangles her matted hair.
A strata of clay clings to her thin rib cage.
Stark white limbs grip the shadows tightly.
She waits, weeping,
knowing the thaw is in her bones.

A Walk on the First Day of Spring

I follow the fenceline
down to the old Preston farm.
There in between the quiet places
is a narrow lane overgrown with shadows
where all the Nebraska seasons
meet for coffee and gossip.

Dry leaves rustle and tumble
over crusts of stale snow.
Vibrant green shoots through
tangled and pungent ditches.
I smell the damp rot of the past
and the stirring of the earth.

The plains release a gusty cry
like that of a ruddy newborn,
pushing winter's last breath
from among the trees.
I stand at the confluence of yesterday and tomorrow,
and it speaks redemption to my soul.

Backyard Cathedral

Hope is the robin
that roves and flits
from apse to nave to altar.
Her feet ignore the cold marble truth
splashing boldly into the baptistry.
She redefines my house of worship,
and I praise Him from my kitchen window.

Storm of 2020

The grove turns as one to the southeast
trunks twisting, limbs creaking,
backbones plastered with abrupt March snow.

Just yesterday, all hours full of life,
sap quickening
buds plump

as the robins in this stark landscape.
Jackrabbits scatter tracks
in the social distance between trees.

All will bide and abide
this northwest bluster
until released to stretch
to unfurl
to pulse with May plain song.

New Poem

I didn't know
that when I bumped into you
a word would break loose

that it would multiply
and take shape
filling a void beneath my soul

at first unrecognizable
but then becoming something
acknowledged, accepted

it swelled and sapped my strength
devoured my days
stole my nights

until one morning
it gushed forth amidst pain and tears
fully formed and full of life

I held it tenderly
overwhelmed that we
had any part

in its beautiful rhythm
perfect lines
pleasing sounds

I cradled it at my breast
vowing to nurture and correct
to affix it in the album of my future

This Morning

the clouds are wispy eyelashes
fluttering against the horizon,
sweeping stardust
from blushing cheeks,

guarding secrets
of a thumbnail moon,
already a whisper
from the night before.

They stretch,
yawn across the sky,
and are now
fully awake.

Spring Thaw

Grandma sorts through her seeds:
lettuce, peas, radish, potatoes.
Soon spring's tender touch
will quiet winter's bluster,
calm fall's neglect,
and brush away last year's tangle
of stalks and leaves.
Her garden bare and beckoning,
her hands shaking,
she will work the soil
mixing snowmelt and sun,
and like generations before,
kneel down to plant her dreams.

A Hepburn Sunrise

The Boeing 737
threads the clouds
like a silver needle threads pearls,
stringing together
an elegant necklace
to adorn the fleshy pink horizon.

Country Church

Your clapboard siding,
peeling and chapped,
like skinned knees after a fall,
or lips without a prayer.

The stained-glass windows,
now gaping holes,
leave your heart and soul
exposed and wild.

Pigeons, not liturgy,
fill the rafters,
their chorus a cappella,
while mice build nests in the organ.

Your spire resolute,
its shadow a timepiece for the dead.
Rows upon rows of saints,
never late for Matins or Vespers.

Backs stiff and proud,
gaudy flowers in their hats,
eternally chanting
"*Te Deum Laudemus*" or "*Magnificat.*"

And with the Benediction,
their long shadows
stretch into the aisles,
shaking hands and exchanging peace.

Gray Morning

A young doe
breaks free
from an endless palette of green.

A dappled brown
that suddenly jolts
this rainy landscape into being.

Just Another Day

Golden sunrise kisses the horizon
spreading warmth from hill to valley.
Tender breezes caress the land
awakening trees, fields, gardens.
Branches stretch, embrace the sky.
Cornstalks flirt with birds and bees.
Flowers lift up their faces, smiling.

Thin clouds creep across the sky,
shadows skitter from hill to hill.
The sun's promises fade
as a chill settles in the furrows and ditches.
Air so heavy and tense
the land can't help but hold its breath.

A cold hard gust slams the hills
stripping trees and stalks of their souls
(limbs crash to the ground.)
Blackness rolls over the land,
jolts of anger and light strike.
Bruising, ripping, breaking.
Wind and cloudburst hide the shaking
smother the scream
muffle the harsh flood of words
until suddenly

All is calm.
The sun pierces the darkness,
bright and gentle
with its affected apology.
Battered faces lift toward the light
as shadows slide away.
"Yes, forgiven," their leaves whisper
in the tender breeze,
golden sunset kiss.

Chance of Rain

You wind me up like an old hose,
pulling me slowly toward home.
You work out my kinks
and coil me at your feet.
All that I am, stacked like the backbone
of a farmer toiling for the certain unknown.
My eyes leak for tomorrow.
You lift my face to the sky
where hope billows on the horizon.
I will thirst no more.

Rope Burn

These rope swing days of summer
swaying long and lazy
waves of heat
bare feet
tracing circles in the dust

Maple branches creaking
locusts singing
forgotten husks clinging
to all things
frayed

Hazy hours lean back and dip
sweaty grip
slips through time
blistered and chafed
middle of July

Thunderstorm in July

It woke me at 4 a.m.
Petulant raindrops,
a fitful sigh through the trees,
uncertain of its surroundings,
weary of the heat.

Clouds blanketed the fields,
bunched and twisted.
A whimper, a rustle,
limbs begin to flail
as the wind groaned.

Then with light flashing,
thunder kicking and rolling,
it wailed and wept until spent.
Asleep on its earthy bed,
the fever broken.

And Then Truth

Young and confident
she stood tall in the grove
her limbs lithe and free
intent on reaching the stars
her strength green and presumptuous.

Then life grew up around her
closing her in
seasons changed, storms raged
her bark thickened, her limbs sagged
her leaves bled out and dropped like gossip.

Until one calm night
she fell.
And those that noticed
commented on how hollow she was
and how, for all these years,
had she stood at all?

Insomnia

It was dead. Gone.
Buried deep.
But as the flesh fell off the memories
stark truths emerged.
Bones that come together and ride through my dreams.
Past and present become the same,
and the night is forever.

September Memories

The wind
flippant,
cruel,
gives flight to a cornhusk.
Like a hollow dream
it spins and twirls,
stretching up,
almost fulfilled —
then out of breath,
it settles back into the dust of reality.

Center Pivot

Her rusty spine
sunbathes on a beach
of brittle stalks,
every vertebra stiff
with sweat and grime
from running circles all summer.

Now October laps at her ribs,
rustling husks
sifting dust
rolling her to rest
in the empty furrows,
alone under the harvest moon.

After Harvest

When the rush of farmers fade,
the clouds of dust settle,
and the hazy red sun bleeds out,
will we even remember
how the crops clung
to the land's contours?
how the heavy air
dripped from husk and silk?
how the leaves winked
in the breeze?
or will we default to rough stubble,
gray plains and bleary eyes?
like old women who love
their men through the seasons.

As the Truck Passed

the old dirt road exhaled slowly
its breath rolling over
sloping shoulders and pitted ditches
and into the ragged creases and folds
of the stale valley
settling low and heavy
like a nagging cough.

Tumbleweed

Until late summer this fenceline was my life
and now cut free
I search for something to hold on to

Last night the wind picked up
strong and convincing
it tumbled me

Rootless and brittle
desperate to find a safe place
I yielded

It scattered my intentions
numbed my reserve
blinded me with flurries of white

Unable to fight this relentless squall
I am sucked into the maelstrom
of gusts and snow

I trip over fields and gullies
catch in branches and barbwire
any hope tattered and cold

I collide with a cornstalk.
Held tight by that steadfast remnant of harvest
I cling to the one who gave it all up
and finally find rest in a season of fallow

Old Plow

Time sifts through the spokes
of your frozen iron wheels,
bound by brome with roots
that run deeper than depression.

Evergreen giants,
with their stiff arms,
push your rusty frame
against the bitter dust of the past.

You slump forward in your
reddish brown coat,
a mantle of sweat and tears,
too much moisture and not enough

shelter from the winds of change.
This belt tightens with
trees planted straight and true,
like the furrows you turned

from Finn's pasture fence
stretching southeast
down to the creek
that ran past Sahs's barn.

That harvest gone, along with
years of both want and plenty.
Only you remain in this season,
forever tilling up memories.

Cornstalk Bales

Cold steel fingers
rake me over the furrows
piling my bones
hustling my memories.

Tumbled, bundled, coiled tight,
I roll out into the thin November air
and exhale,
fully empty.

Unresolved Realities

I walk upon this wintry night
Sunset on my left
Moon overhead
Twice the heavenly light

Yet a feeling of dread
As darkness encroaches
Blackening the shadows
Foreshadowing the blackness

While hope sinks
I continue on this country road
Cutting right down the center
Of thrashed and winnowed spaces

Wide open and free
Yet imprisoned with twisted barbs
Heart full of promise
Yet emptied of its plenty

I walk upon this wintry night
Going somewhere and nowhere

Maple Leaf

I walk aimlessly this cold November morning,
eyes and heart unable to lift up from the ground.
I notice you, laying there amongst the others,
your veins enhanced by the heavy frost,
your golden flesh forlorn, exhaling bitterness
beneath the indifferent tree.
My eyes trace the unforgiving bark to glorious heights.
So many strong branches
that held you,
sheltered you,
nourished you.
And then, like a changing season, the tree withdrew,
leaving you to spin helpless in the wind.
So, you gave up,
let go,
and fell away.
Oh, sweet maple leaf!
Don't you know your worth?
The tree may not want you anymore,
but I do.
I pluck you from the pile of forsaken dreams,
and tuck you between the pages of mine.

First Blizzard

We have been waiting all day,
gazing out the window,
looking over our shoulders to the north,
as tri-state warnings resound.

We are charged and tense,
like the air around us,
detained like the grove of trees,
their last leaves, quivering, ready to bolt.

Then, just as the weatherman foretold,

the wind bears down,
the sky tilts and bursts forth,
piercing the hills,
erasing the horizon.

Time blurs and grows dim.
Our grip on winter's armchair relaxes.
Busy lives drift over.
Now we are free.

Generations

A great gust of snow
swirls and blows across the plain
startling a flock of blackbirds
from the warm folds of the field.

It's a comforting cloud of black,
earthy and familiar,
with its choreographed lift, reverse loop,
and steady landing back among the stalks.

And now strutting about,
in and out,
solidly flustered,
an undulating cluster of thoughts
and age-old schemes.

Maybe we all get a bit ruffled
as we abide nature's reproach.
Yet we keep doing what we know
in this land we live on.

Midwest Winter

It blew in on a nor'wester weeks ago.
Got itself stuck in every prickly branch,
like a plastic bag in the tree across the street.

Straining against its captors,
it grew frantic and more tangled.
(It kept you up at night with its flapping.)

Until, exhausted, it sank into a cold gray stupor,
pressing out the present,
suffocating us all.

If only I could climb high enough,
loosen the trees' twisted grip,
this synthetic heaven would whirl and drift away.

Its stranglehold released,
we would gulp down the bright blue air,
exhaling this stale winter existence.

New Year's Song

I rise from the ashes of a war-torn year,
blinking against the grit,
lips dry with the dust of appeals.

I move through the rubble of resolve,
past jagged dreams and promises,
collapsed under the weight of their pretense.

I pull this blanket of hope tighter,
although torn and tattered,
its warmth my strength.

I lift my eyes toward a single voice,
its melody brushing aside
dusty motes of mistakes.

A trill of anticipation,
a call to move forward,
to spark a revolution.

January Fog

This cold, gray earth,
no hint of breath or beat,
must have frozen in its sleep.
So, without hesitation
or coroner's consent,
thick, heavy fog
enfolds the countryside
like a loose shroud.
Whether well-off or dirt poor,
all are draped in the same burial linen,
a wintry Lazarus
awaiting the voice of spring.

Early Praise for *Fencelines*

Stimulating and graceful, these poems will create in readers imagined visions based on the author's vivid descriptions of life and beauty overlooked by most others. *Fencelines* is a big-hearted treasure for any enthusiast of poetic words.

— Alan J. Bartels, former editor, *Nebraska Life Magazine*

Like William Stafford did for the Kansas fields, Angela Hansen has taken the Nebraska countryside and helped us see the magic and meaning that is imbued therein."

— Susan McDowall, English instructor
Central Community College, Grand Island, NE

Fencelines is a body of work encapsulating Hansen's personal journey of self-preservation and growth, "where all the Nebraska seasons meet for coffee and gossip." Hansen exhibits the resilience of womanhood among the prairie. Her poems read like Polaroids; she carries her readers through colorful snapshots of her personal love, loss, pain, and acceptance, all nestled between vivid, organic imagery of an unforgiving, yet fruitful countryside existence. Every poem in Hansen's collection embodies cathartic release.

— Sharon Nicole Carr, Adult Services librarian,
Wayne Public Library

About the Author

Angela Hansen was born and raised in the farmland of northeast Nebraska. She spent her childhood immersed in family and everything outside: the grove of trees, the crooked bridge down by the creek, and the surrounding countryside. Angela attended country school through 8th grade, graduated from Wayne High School, and received a bachelor's degree in English Writing from Wayne State College. Her dream of writing and illustrating children's books was overcome with the practicality of working steady jobs, which over the years included librarian, assistant manager of a bookstore, baker at a college coffee shop, paraoptometric, paraprofessional at an elementary school, and presently, running her own business as a house painter.

Angela lived in St. Louis, MO, and LaGrange Park, IL, before moving back to Nebraska. She bought an acreage outside Carroll, where she lives with her three children, four goats, and a Ridgeback mix puppy. She enjoys baking, woodworking, gardening, creating, and finding just the right word. Her poetry has been published in *Nebraska Life Magazine* and shared at a few readings over the years.

Angela considers her faith in God the only reason she survived over 16 years of domestic violence and why she continues to heal, to find beauty in the world, and joy in her farmer and their kids.

About The Poetry Box®

The Poetry Box®, a boutique publishing company in Portland, Oregon, provides a platform for both established and emerging poets to share their words with the world through beautiful printed books and chapbooks.

Feel free to visit the online bookstore (thePoetryBox.com), where you'll find more titles including:

The Catalog of Small Contentments by Carolyn Martin

Built to Last by Tara L. Carnes

What Is Not a Miracle by Don Badgley

Bee Dance by Cathy Cain

A Long, Wide Stretch of Calm by Melanie Green

Of the Forest by Linda Ferguson

Let's Hear It for the Horses by Tricia Knoll

Stronger Than the Current by Mark Thalman

Sophia & Mister Walter Whitman by Penelope Scambly Schott

What We Bring Home by Susan Coultrap-McQuin

The Kingdom of Birds by Joan Colby

A Nest in the Heart by Vivienne Popperl

and more . . .

www.ingramcontent.com/pod-product-compliance
Lightning Source LLC
Chambersburg PA
CBHW061706090526
44820CB00034B/2649